Baby's FIRST ABC BOOK

a black and white book

Written and illustrated
Manali Rajvansh

Baby's First ABC Book
Written and illustrated by Manali Rajvansh.

ISBN (paperback) 9789354166426
ISBN(ebook) 9789354193422

First edition - 2020.
Written and Edited by Manali Rajvansh .
Book design and Cover by Manali Rajvansh .
Printed in India.

NOTE TO PARENTS

Why use black and white book?

♥Vision is in fact one of the least developed functions of a newborn's sensory system.Your little one's vision won't catch up to the full capability of an average adult until they are at least 4 years of age.
However our little ones possess the skill of distinguishing between dark and light.

♥ For the first 3 months, your little one will only see around 12 inches from their face, primarily in shades of black, grey and white. Their ability to distinguish the full clarity of colour will only emerge at around 6 months, the first colour they truly distinguish being red at around 3 months.

♥ Black and white images in books causes SENSORY STIMULATION. Sensory stimulation of any kind causes the nerve cells in your little one's brain to multiply and start connecting, and despite everything visual being a little blurry in these early days an incredible 80% of the information newborns absorb comes from what they see.
♥ The nerve cells that are stimulated have a direct pathway to your little one's brain, accelerating their brain growth and improving their ability to concentrate and focus.

♥ The more these nerve cells are stimulated the quicker their brain grows and the faster their visual development, with research repeatedly showing that babies surrounded by the right stimulation reach developmental milestones faster.

Importance of sensory stimulation via black and white images-

1)Helps stimulate optic nerve development.

2)Strong black and white patterns also help babies to develop their ability to focus their attention and levels of concentration.

3)Focusing on such visual stimuli trains newborns' vision, teaching the eye muscles and brain to coordinate and function properly.

4)Engagement with contrasting images, diverse textures and patterns boosts infants learning and focus.

Reference-
https://www.researchgate.net/publication/296716044_The_Visual_World_of_Infants_Discovering_what_babies_can_see_has_been_a_formidable_challenge_but_research_methods_now_provide_an_objective_picture_of_their_surprising_visual_abilities

Dedicated to my son

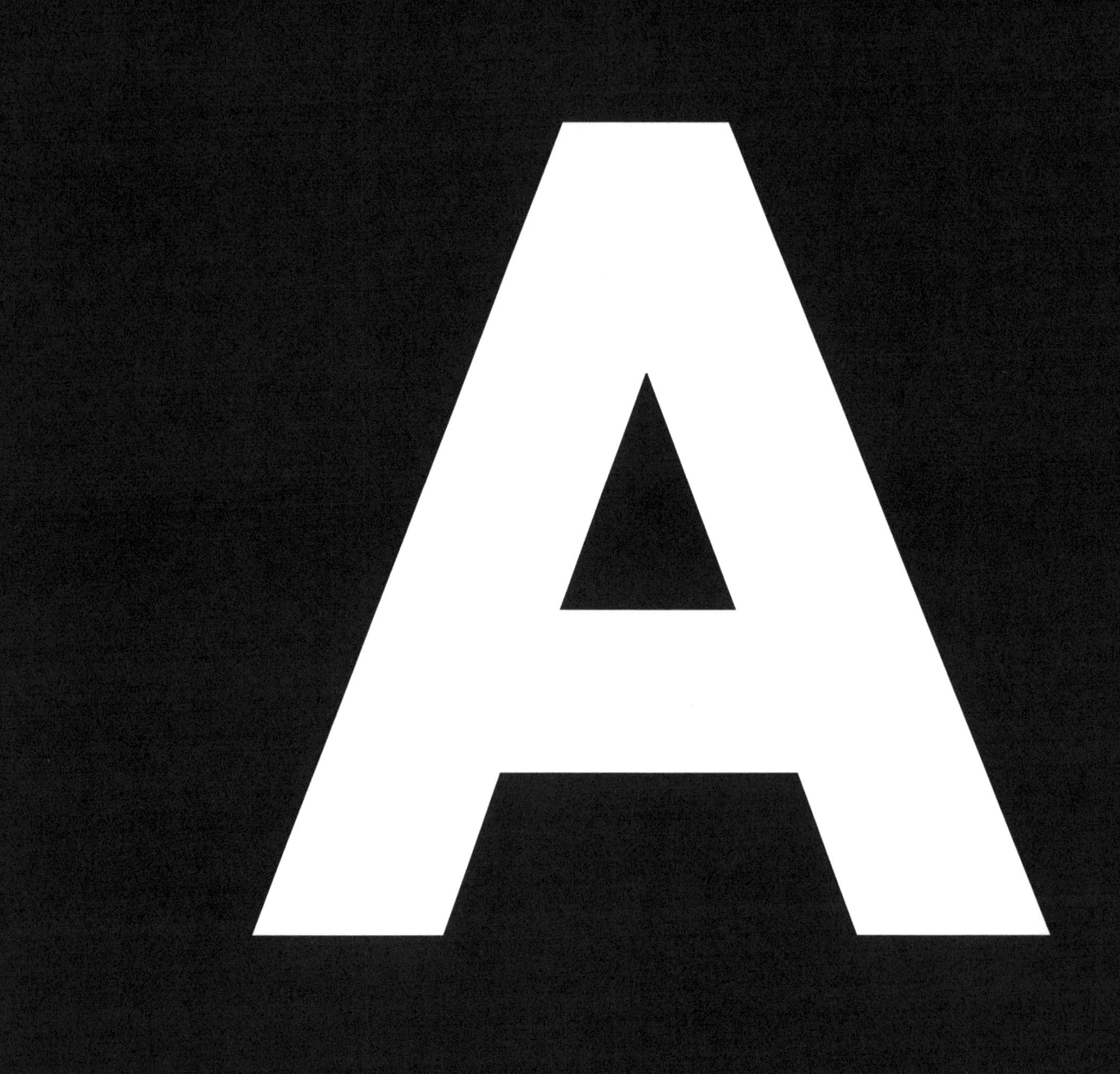

APPLE

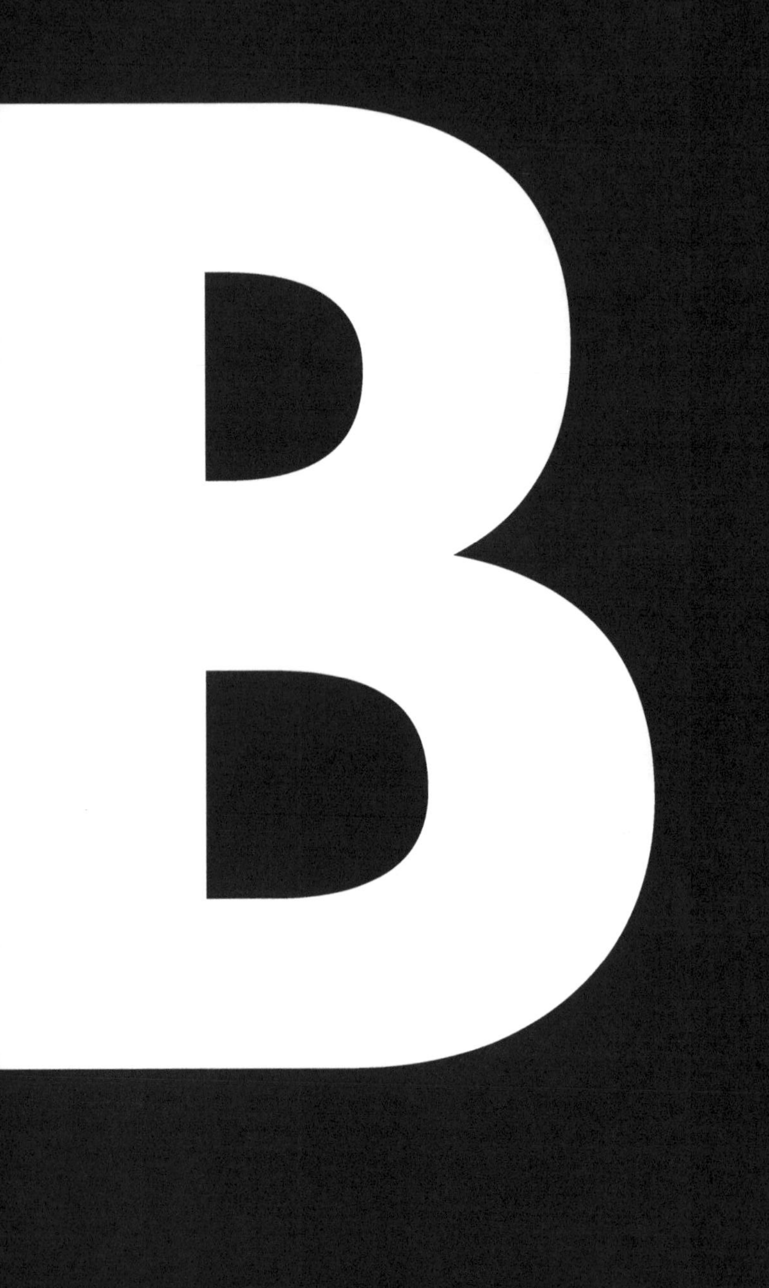

BALL

CAT

DOG

ELEPHANT

FISH

GRAPES

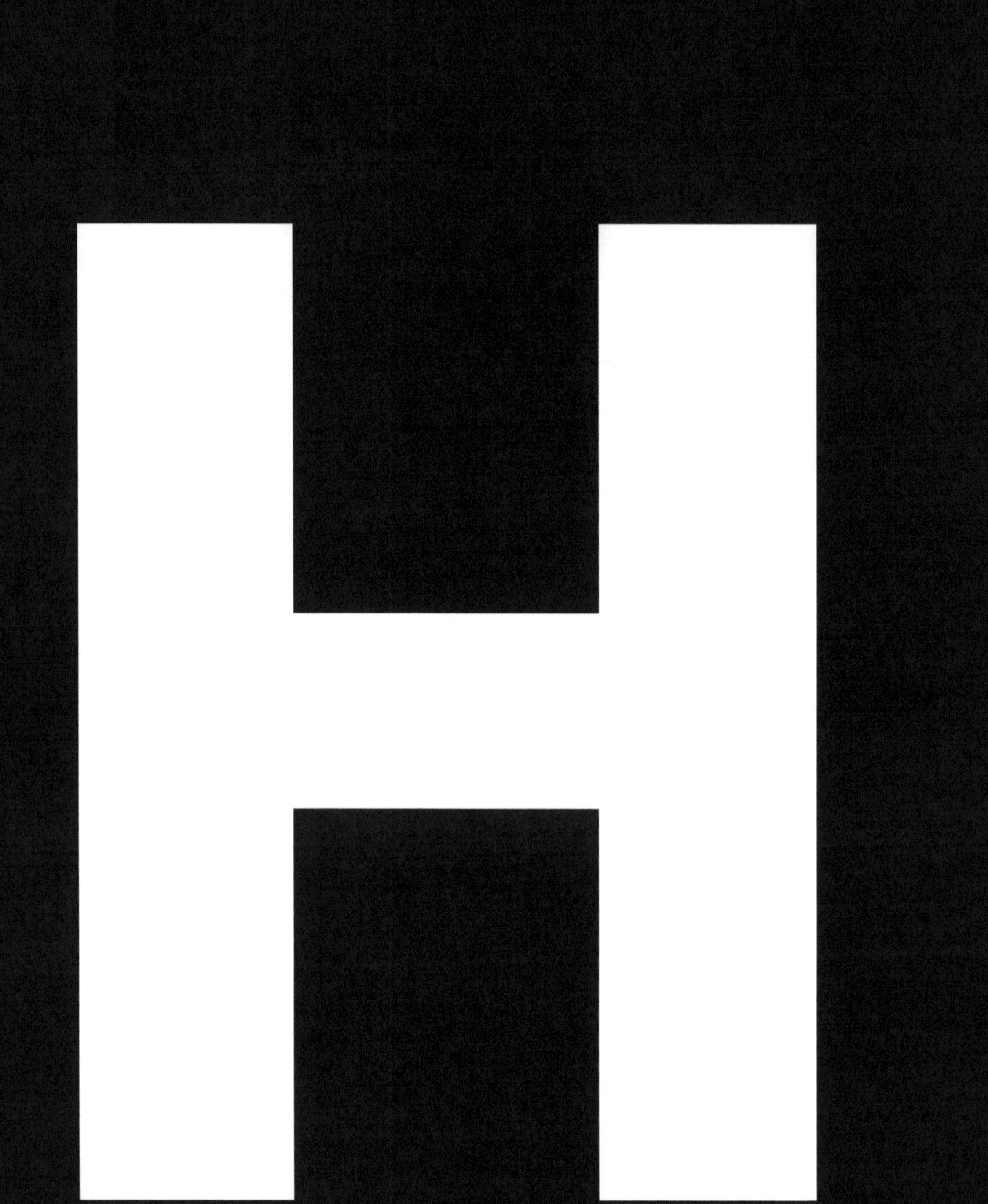

HEN

ICE CREAM

JUG

KITE

LION

M

MONKEY

NEST

ORANGE

PARROT

QUEEN

RABBIT

SUN

TREE

UMBRELLA

VAN

W

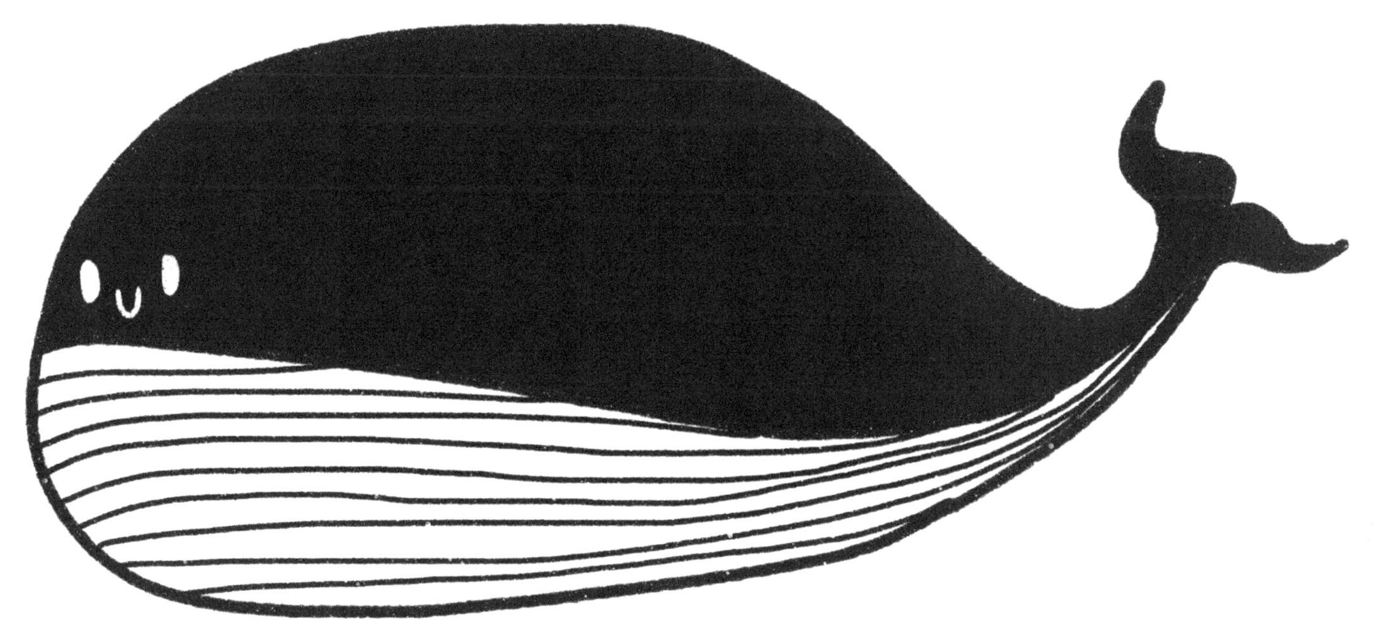

WHALE

XMAS TREE

YAK

Z

ZEBRA

ABOUT THE AUTHOR

Dr. Manali Rajvansh is a consultant oral and dental surgeon by day and writer by night. She lives in India with her husband and son. After getting her Bachelor of dental surgery degree, she discovered that her true passion lies in her writing and illustration.

She has illustrated and published children's picture book "Mischievous Max" and a poetry book "Poet's Yard". Follow her on Instagram @drmanalirajvansh.

www.ingramcontent.com/pod-product-compliance
Lightning Source LLC
LaVergne TN
LVHW071621180726

843512LV00002B/217